HOW IS MY BODY FEELING

Sarah Read

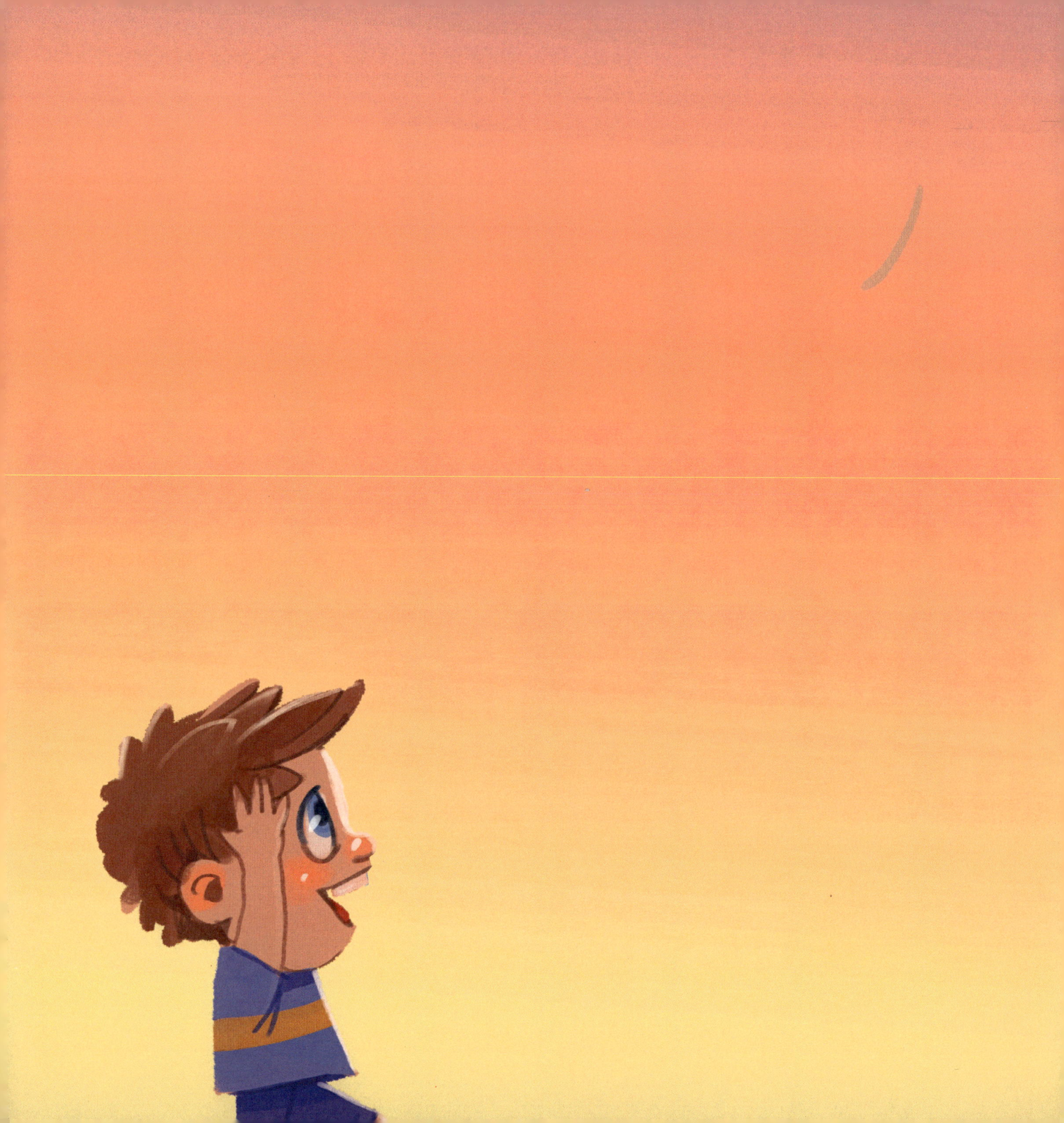

THIS BOOK BELONGS TO

....

....

One day, Archie was outside with his friends hard at play.
He'd been running around in the sun for most of the day.
He noticed that his body was hot, wet and sticky;
He didn't like being sweaty, it made him feel icky.

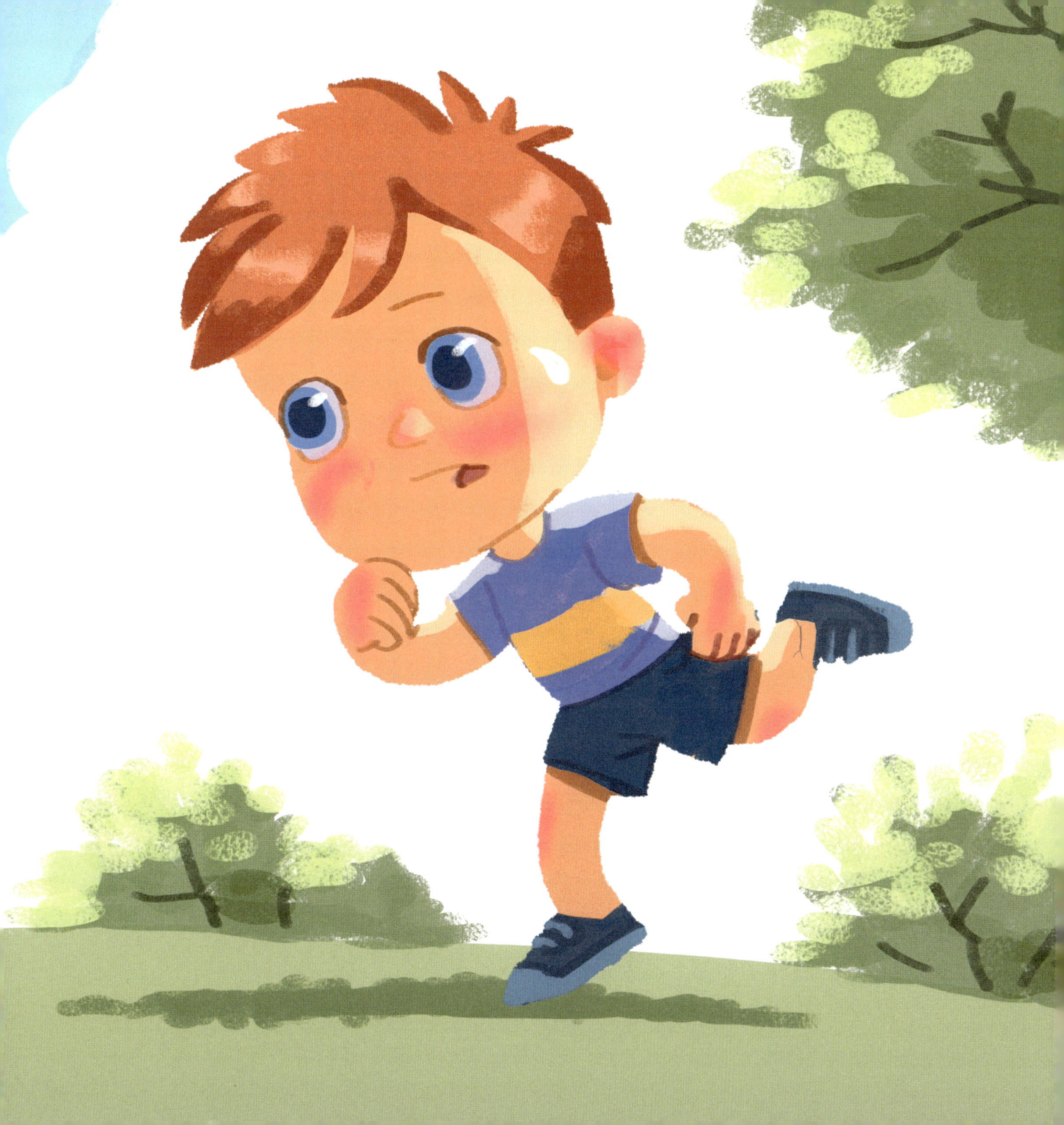

Archie's mouth felt dry — he probably needed a drink.
His head felt so stuffy, it made it hard to think.
He wondered why playing in the sun made him feel this way.
He didn't want to continue; he was done for the day.

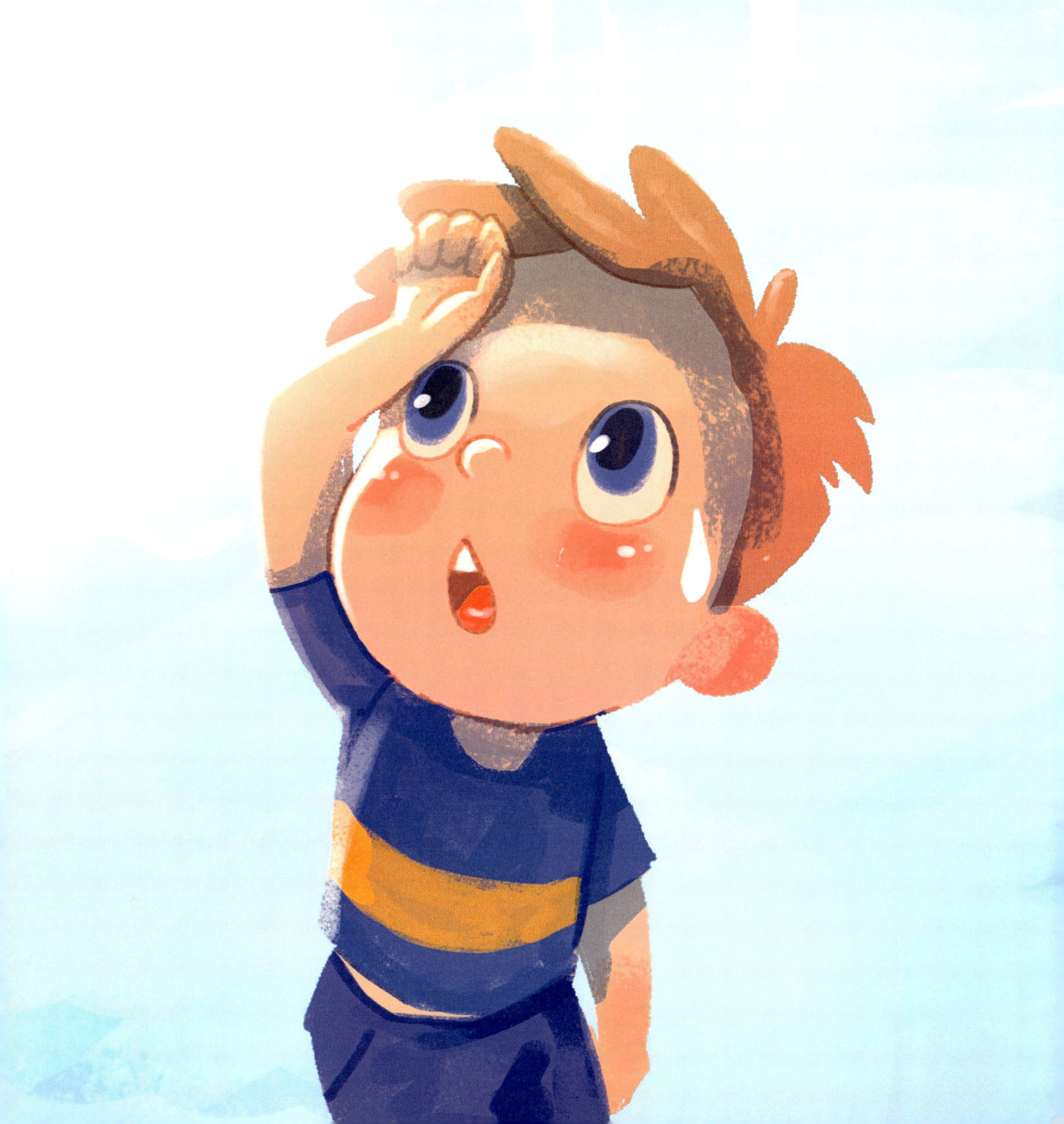

At dinner time, Archie finished cleaning off his plate.
Mom's mac and cheese was his favorite. He thought it was great!.
When Archie was full, he noticed something he'd not yet known.
After a whole plate of mac and cheese, his tummy had grown.

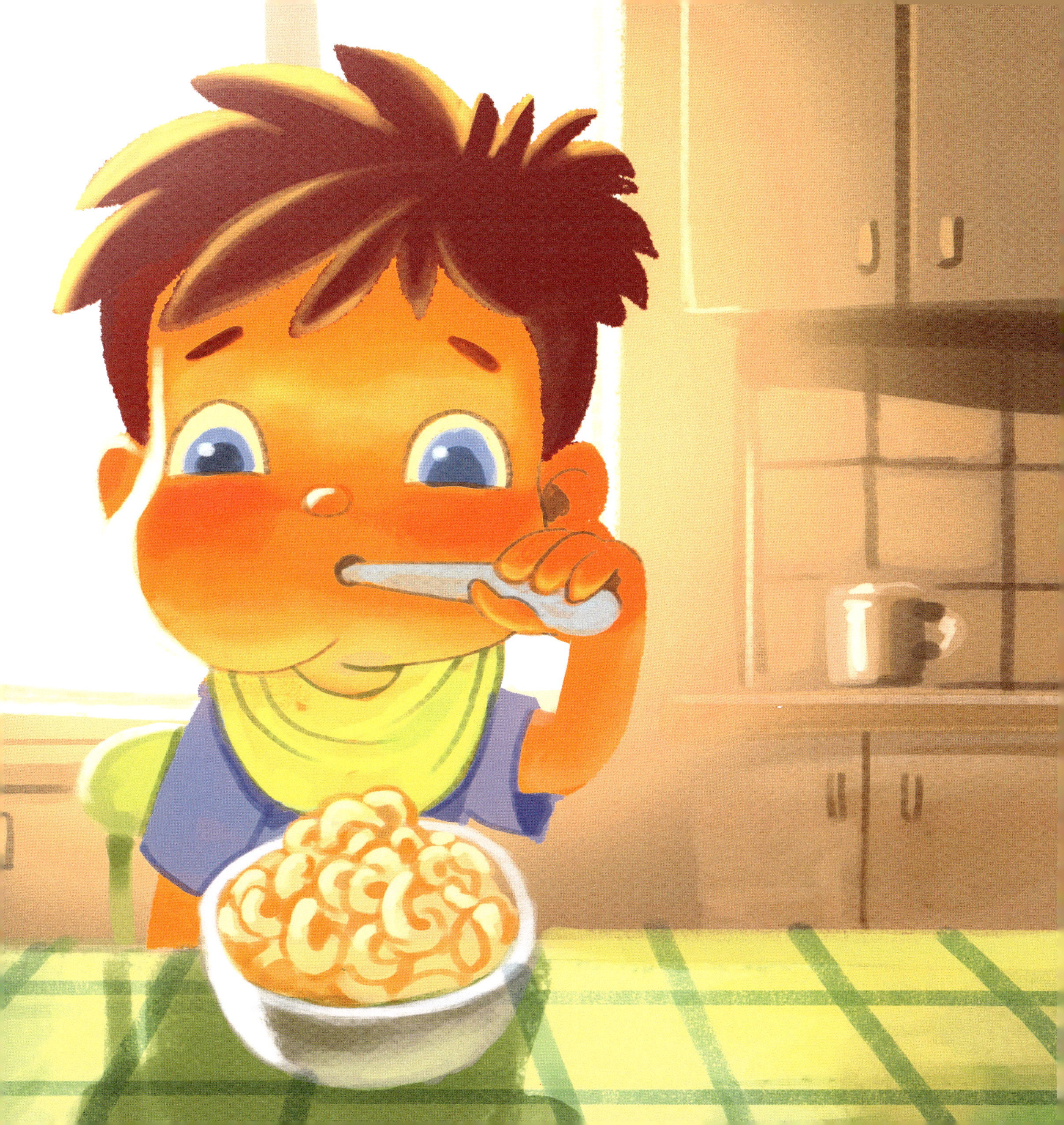

It was like a great big balloon — it didn't feel right.
He undid the button on his pants as they felt very tight.
Why had eating too much made his tummy hard like wood?
Archie loved mac and cheese, but this feeling wasn't good.

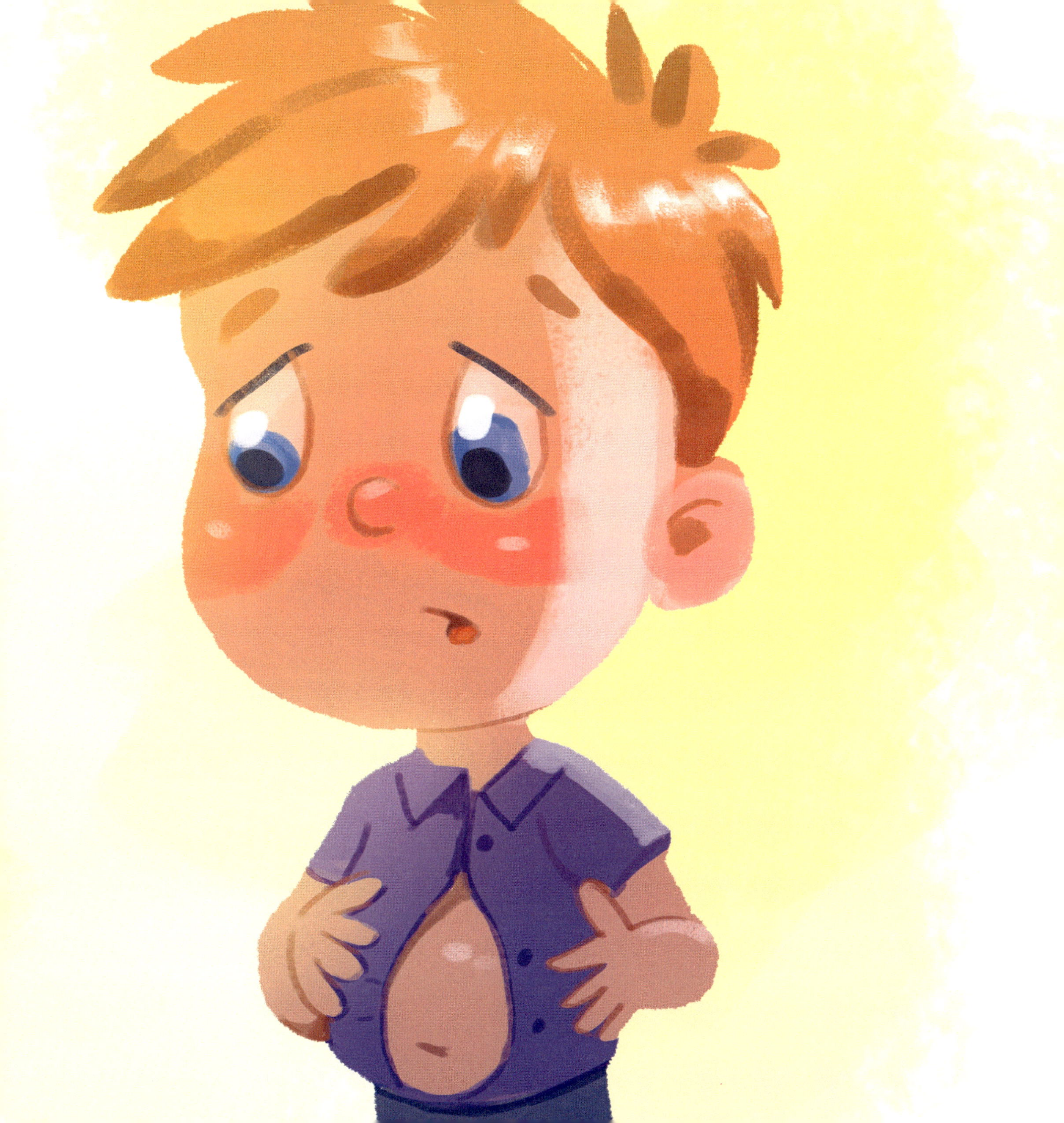

That night, when his dad read a story to him before bed,
Archie yawned and felt sleepy as he cuddled his ted.
Before the story was finished, he could no longer hear
What Dad was reading; sleep was creeping ever near.

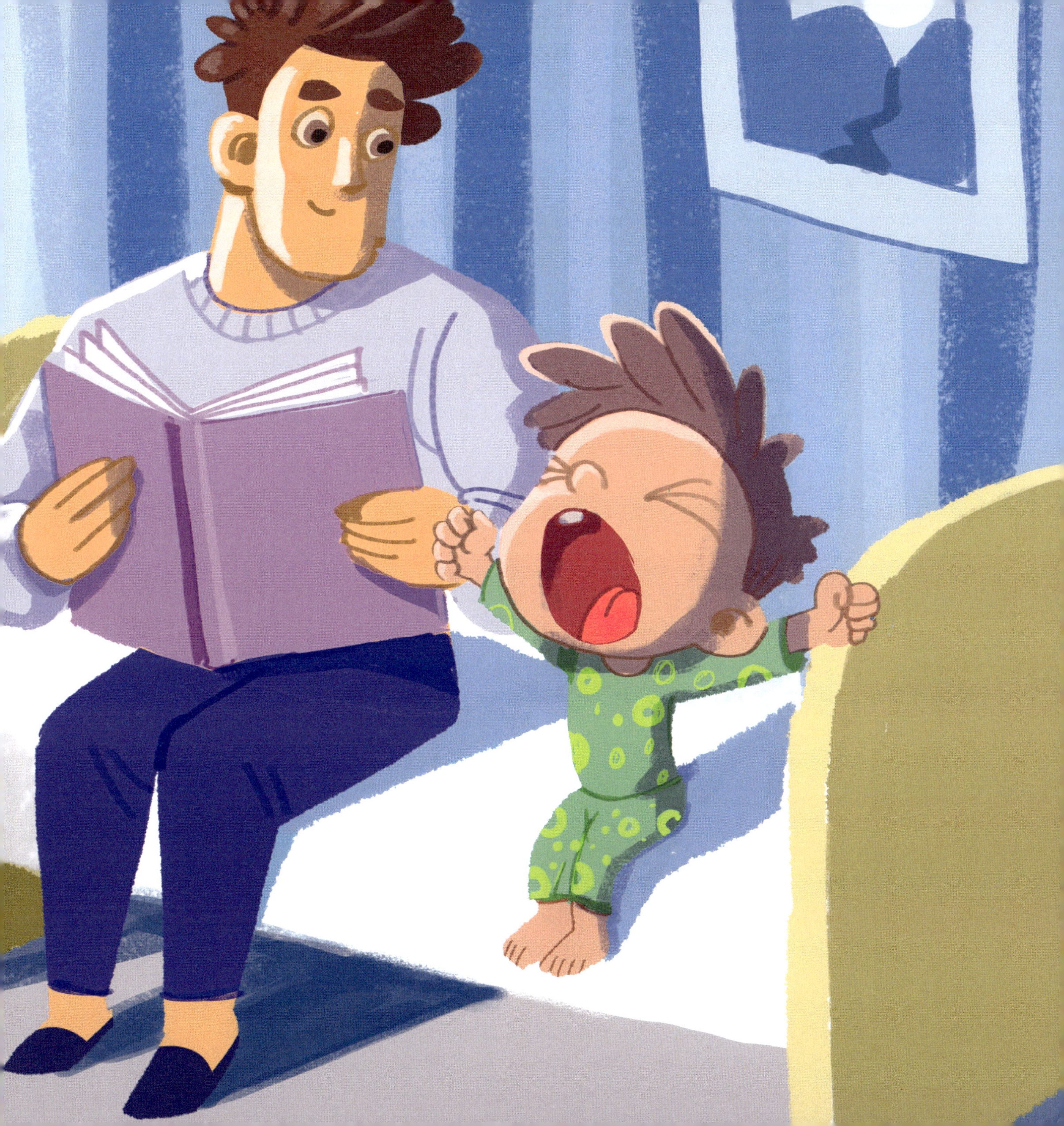

Archie noticed that when things weren't going his way,
His whole body feels hot and it ruins his whole day.
His tummy aches, he breathes faster and his jaw becomes tight.
His hands clench into fists like he's ready fight.

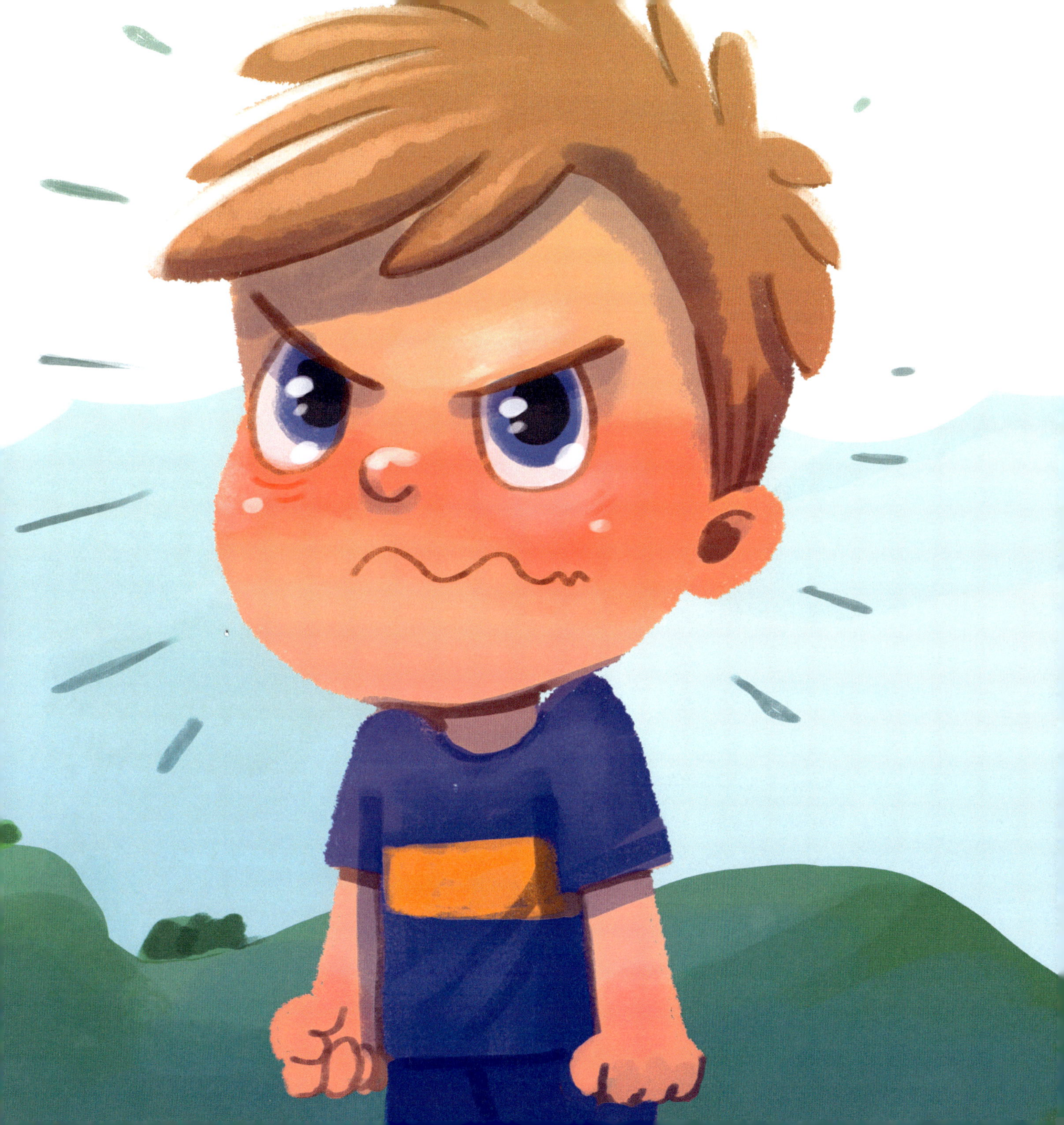

Archie wants to understand so he asked his big sister, May,
About all the sensations he's feeling, especially today.
May remembers odd sensations, she'd felt them at school.
She said, "I was worried I'd mess up my speech and look like a fool."

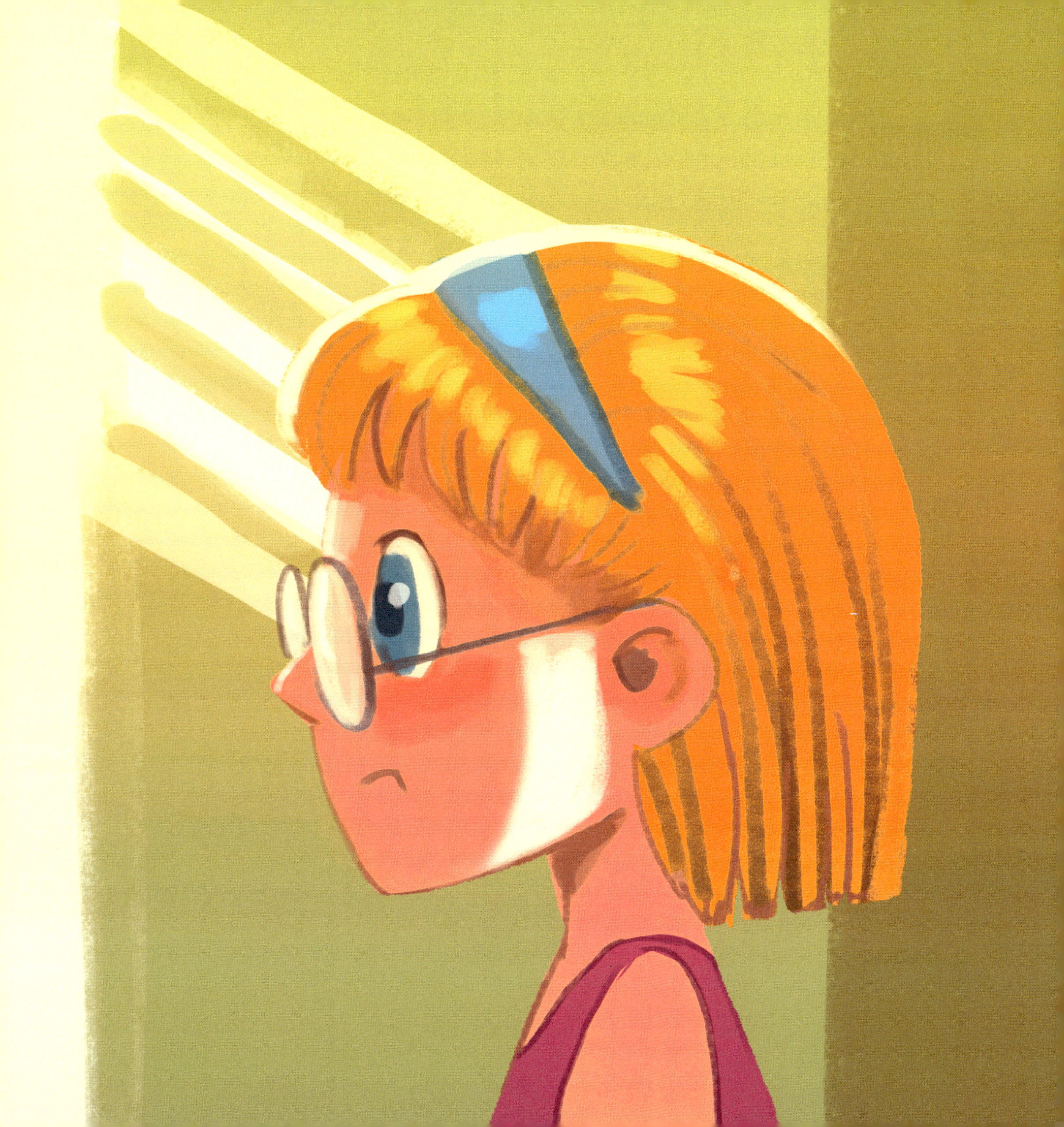

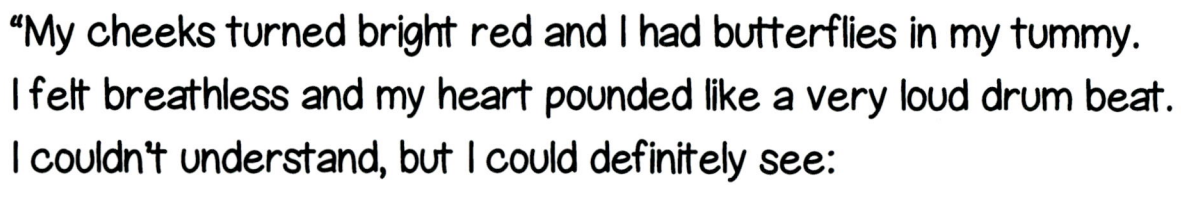

"My cheeks turned bright red and I had butterflies in my tummy.
I felt breathless and my heart pounded like a very loud drum beat.
I couldn't understand, but I could definitely see:
Those sensations meant I was feeling as scared as could be."

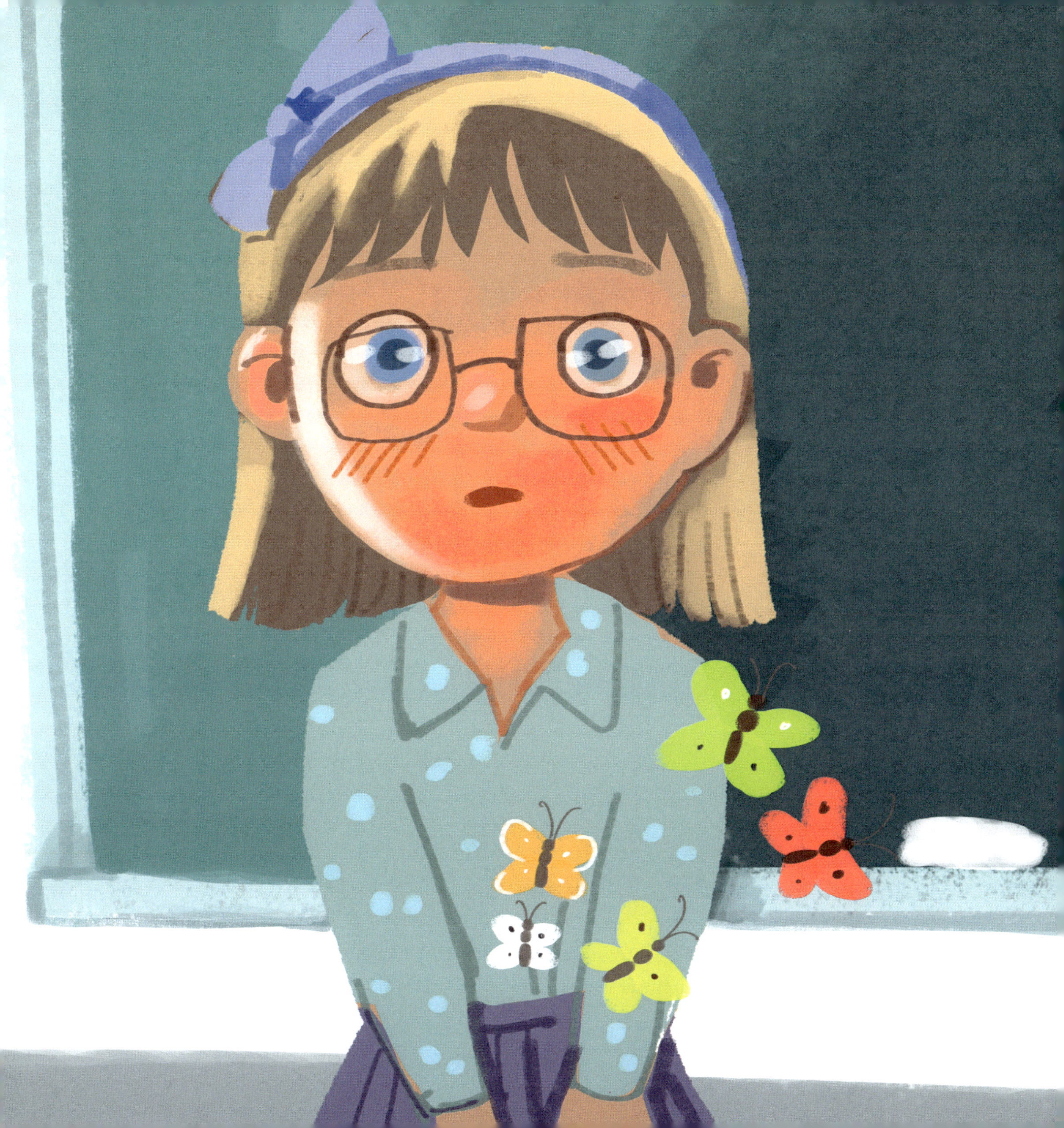

When they went to ask Mom about these sensations, Archie said,
"Some sensations make us smile — some make us angry and red."
"Don't think of them as good or bad," Mom said, "they help you realise
What your body is feeling and might need. Your body is wise."

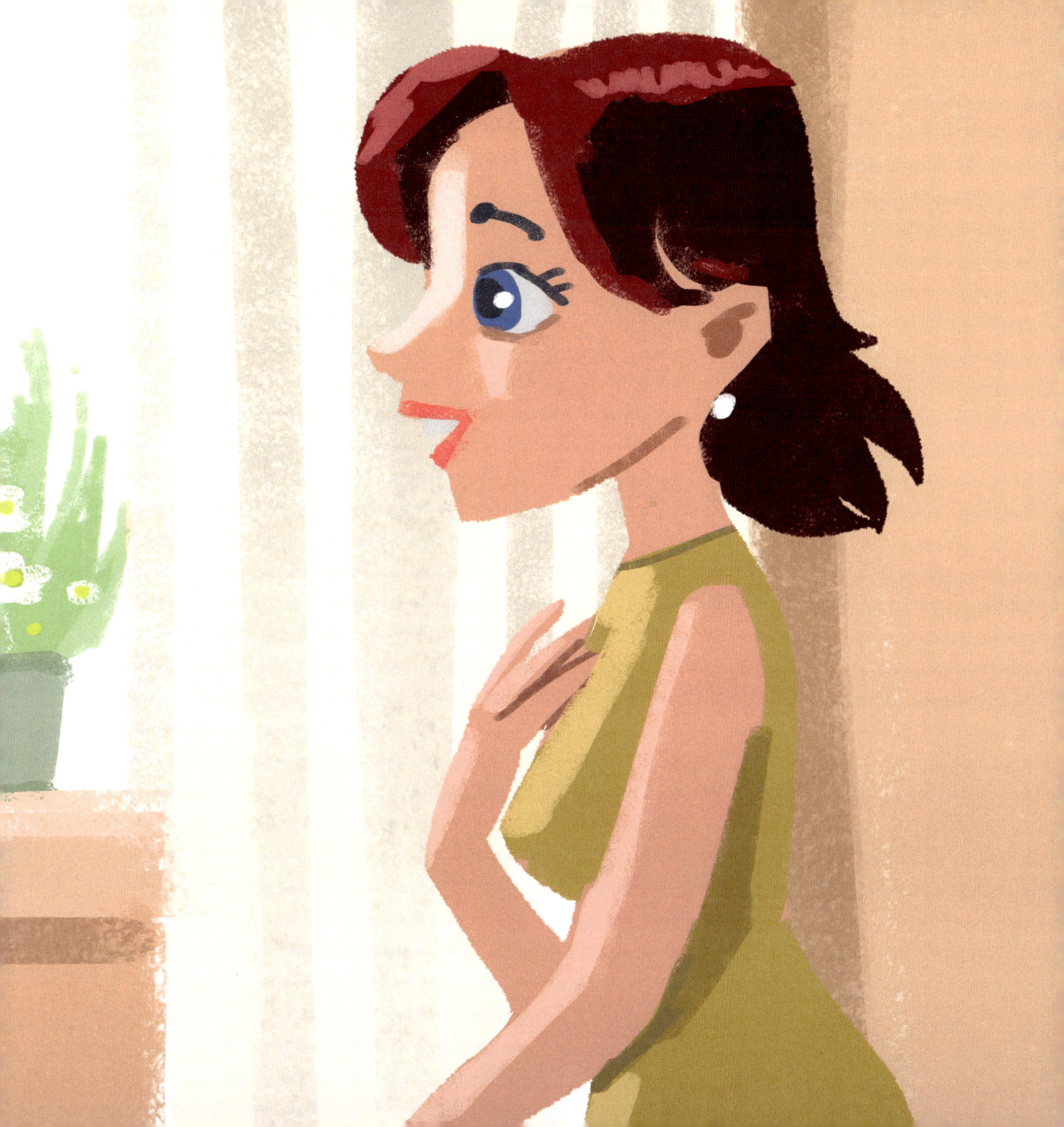

"Pay attention and try to understand. The sensations are clues. Then, the next time they happen," Mom said, "you'll know what to do."

"We'll be sensation-solving detectives — solving mysteries," said May Archie agreed. "Our sensations will guide us throughout every day."

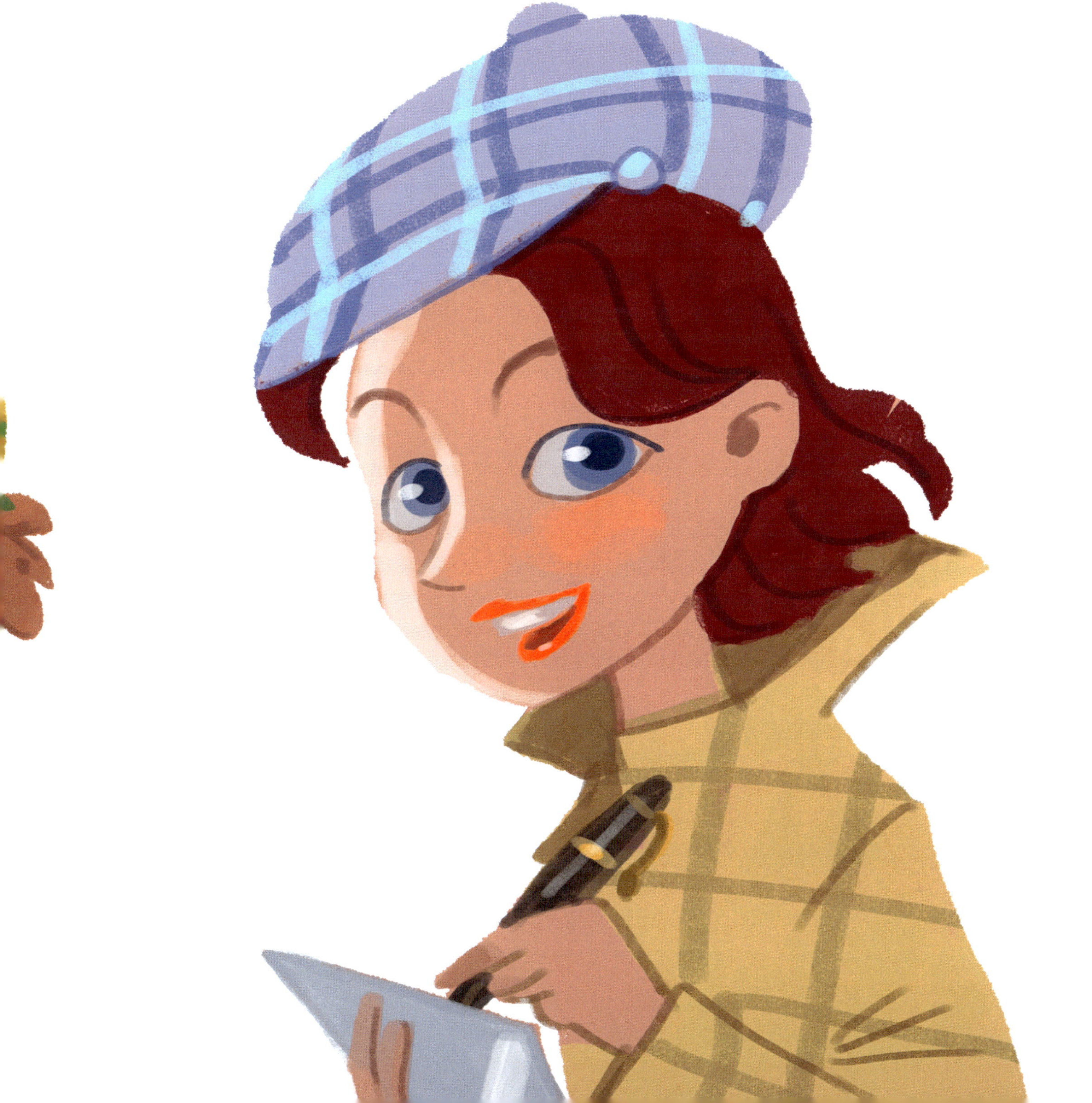

Archie and May are thrilled that they've discovered something new.
They love the way their bodies' sensations tell them what to do.
They're learning to understand all the signals their bodies send.
"I love my body," said Archie and May agreed. "It's like my best friend."

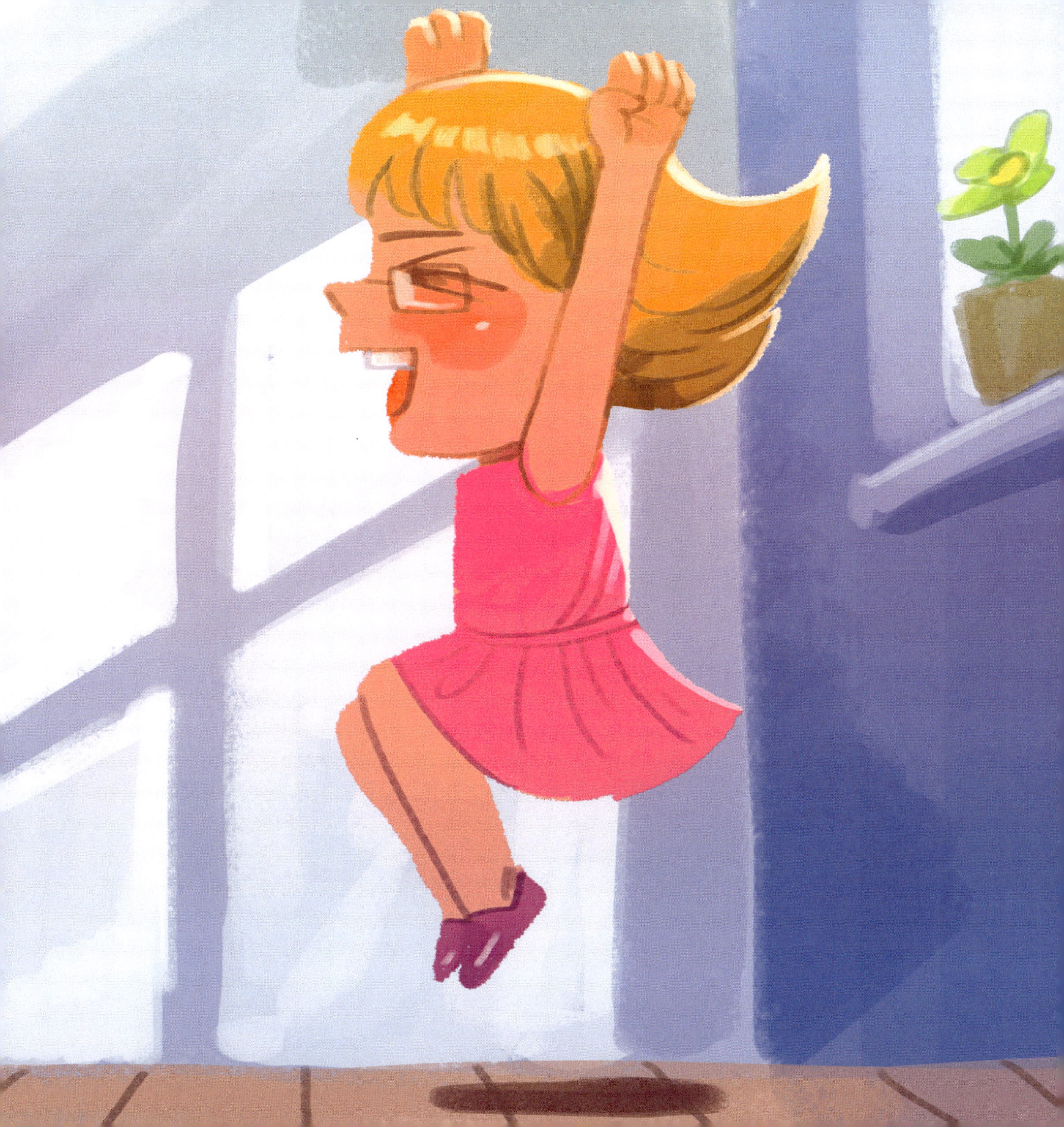

The End

What Did You Think of *How is My Body Feeling?*

Thank you for purchasing this book. I know you could have picked any number of books to read, but you picked this book and for that I am extremely grateful.

If you like the book... and if you'd be willing to spare just two or three minutes...would you be willing to share your review of the book on Amazon?

If you would, it would mean the absolute world to me!

Thank you SO much. This helps to get the book into as many hands as possible, helping other parents and educators!

I really appreciate all your support!

    Sarah Read
    children's book author

Thank you!

⭐⭐⭐⭐⭐

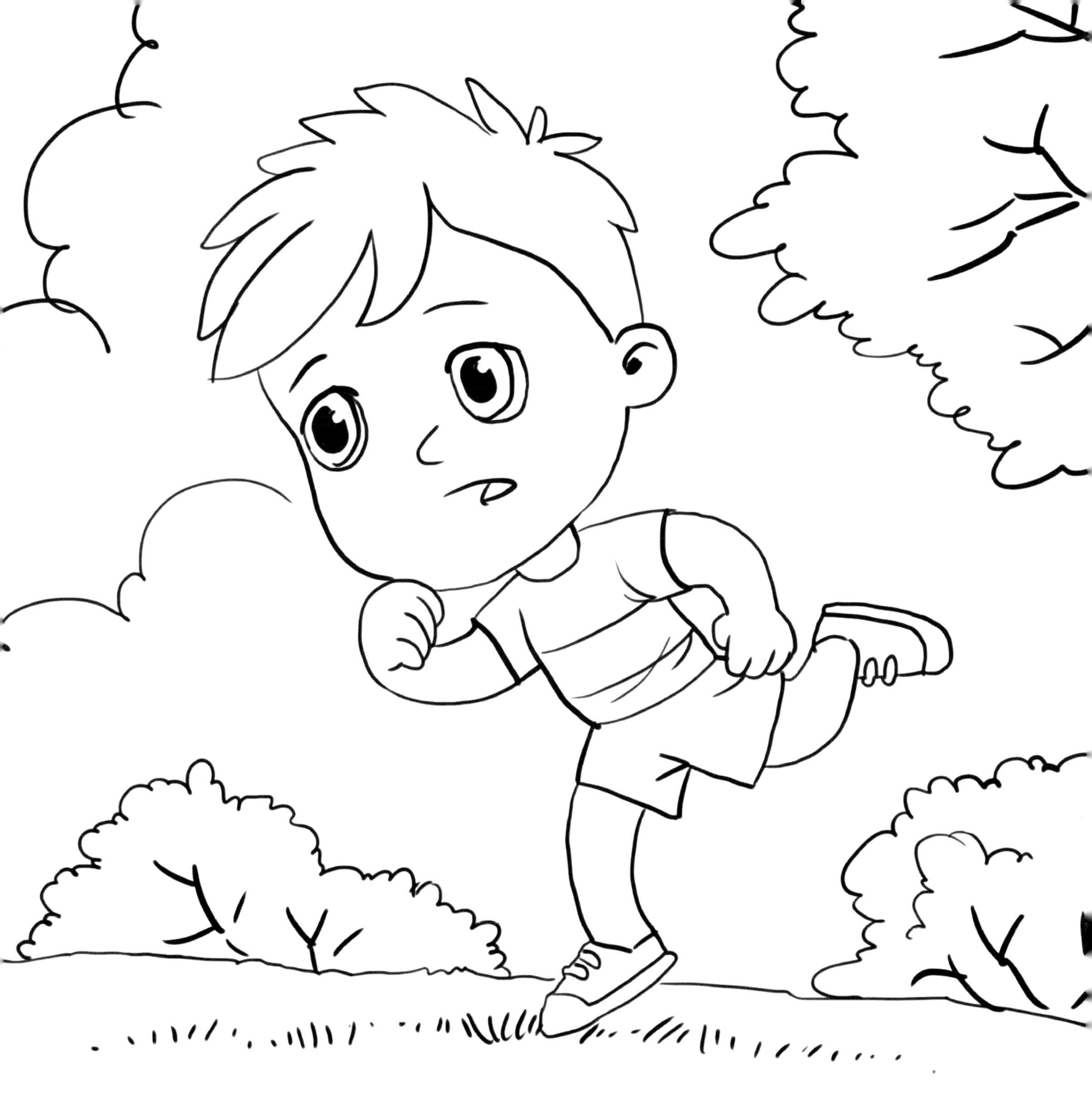

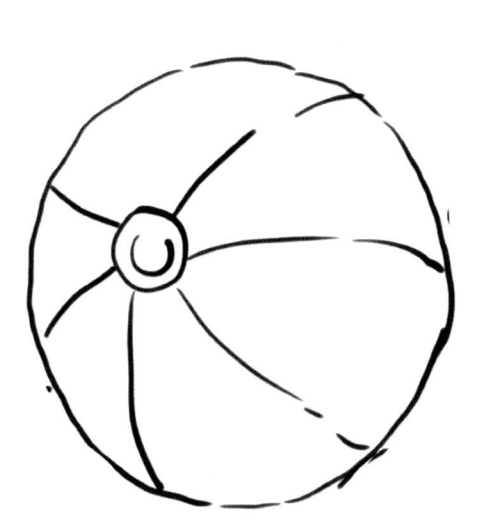

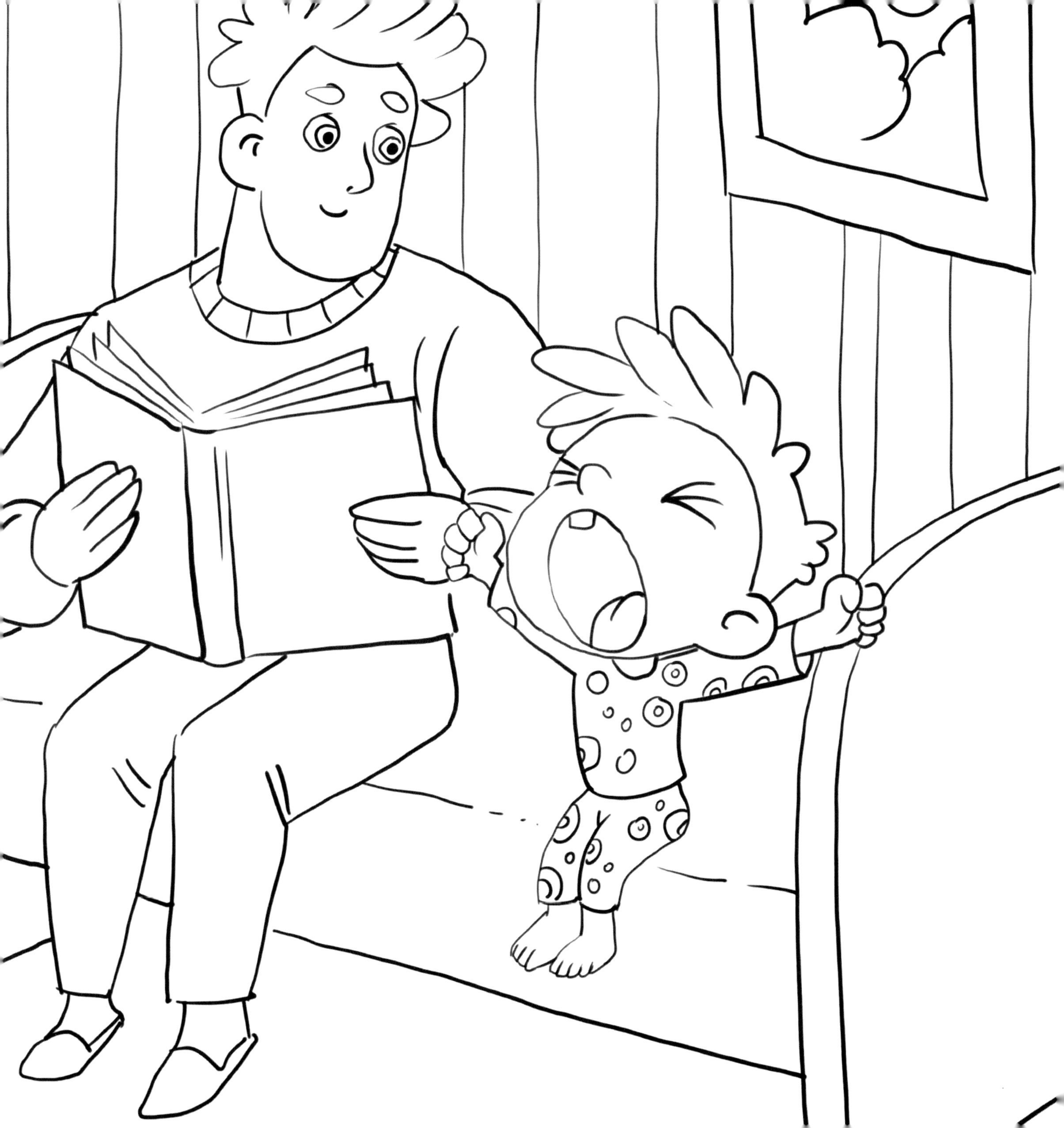

© 2020 Sarah Read. All rights reserved.

All rights reserved. This book or parts thereof may not be reproduced in any form, stored in any retrieval system, or transmitted in any form by any means—electronic, mechanical, photocopy, recording, or otherwise—without prior written permission of the publisher,